D1435693

WITHDRAWN

ACTE

by Lawrence Durrell

NOVELS

The Alexandria Quartet:
   Justine
   Balthazar
   Mountolive
   Clea
The Black Book
Pope Joan (translation)
The Dark Labyrinth

LETTERS

Lawrence Durrell and Henry Miller: A Private Corresponden

TRAVEL

Bitter Lemons
Reflections on a Marine Venus
Prospero's Cell

POETRY

Collected Poems
On Seeming to Presume
The Tree of Idleness

DRAMA

Sappho: a play in verse
An Irish Faustus: a morality in nine scenes
Acte

HUMOUR

Stiff Upper Lip
Esprit de Corps

FOR YOUNG PEOPLE

White Eagles Over Serbia

ACTE

a play by

Lawrence Durrell

New York
E. P. DUTTON & CO., INC.

First published in the U.S.A. 1966
by E. P. Dutton & Co., Inc.

Copyright © 1965 by Lawrence Durrell

Printed in Great Britain

DRAMATIS PERSONAE

PETRONIUS ARBITER

FLAVIA, his niece, wife of Fabius

TESTER, slave

METELLUS, satrap of Scythia

FABIUS, Roman general

TULLUS, a staff officer

ACTE, princess of Scythia

GALBA, councillor

A Nurse

EIRON, a scribe

NERO, the Emperor

A Waiting Maid

SPORUS

A Barber

Ghost of Agrippina appearing to Nero, jailor, slaves, servants, female attendants

SCENES

9

ILLUSTRATIONS

Four photographs of the production of the play in German by Gustav Gründgens at the Deutsches Schauspielhaus in Hamburg in November 1961 will be found at the end of the book.

The photographs are by Rosemarie Clausen.

ACT ONE/SCENE ONE

The vineyard on the country estate of PETRONIUS. *He is discovered pruning his vines. He is a huge brawny man with a voice of gravel. He pauses to groan and rub his tired back; he blows his nose. He is working by the light of a torch, held by a slave.*

PETRONIUS One more and we're done. Hey!
    (*He claps his hands and another* SLAVE *enters*)
    I'm on the last one now; give me more light.
    (*Second* SLAVE *moves the torch nearer, sets it down and exits. As* PETRONIUS *bends again enter* FLAVIA, *his niece, between two servants holding torches*)

FLAVIA Uncle, what on earth are you doing out here?

PETRONIUS Why, Flavia; is it you?

FLAVIA I've just arrived. This minute.
    Darling, why are you out here?
    You'll catch a chill.

PETRONIUS Dressing the last vines before the moon turns.
    Did you bring the boy?

FLAVIA Yes. We hoped to stay a while, if you'll have us.

PETRONIUS Good. Good. Tester!
    (*Enter* SLAVE)
    Finish this last one, will you?

SLAVE Yes, master.

PETRONIUS And is Fabius with you?

FLAVIA No. Have you heard nothing, then? Nothing at all?
    Living so far from Rome I suppose you get no news.
    No, Fabius has crossed over with the twelfth legion.

PETRONIUS Over what? Over where?

FLAVIA Scythia! A new revolt broke out.
    He's gone to put it down. O, come, you *must* have heard.

PETRONIUS Now I think of it, there was a rumour. Hum.
    So they've started up again, the Scythians?

It's funny, I've been writing a story about such a
thing . . .

FLAVIA Ah! You and your stories.

PETRONIUS Perhaps I provoked it, who knows?
(*He laughs harshly, wiping his hands*)
And it turns upon someone rather like Fabius, too.
You didn't go with him this time? No,
I left you at home too, in the story. You see? Second-
sight!

FLAVIA No, I didn't go with him.
There is no mystery about it.
(*She hangs her head sadly, making a little gesture of
hopelessness*)

PETRONIUS Well, well.
(*He takes her hands sympathetically*)
It hasn't gone very well, has it, Flavia?

FLAVIA It never did. You know that.
Now worse than ever.
(*She sighs*)

PETRONIUS But the boy is all right, isn't he?
That's something. That's everything.

FLAVIA Yes, he's sleeping. Uncle, I have this for you, from the
Palace.
(*She hands him a letter which he takes with a grunt and a
grimace*)

PETRONIUS I can guess what it is.
It's the third this month.
What does poor Nero want with me?

FLAVIA It's very dangerous not to obey, Uncle.
Specially these days.

PETRONIUS Ach! I had things to do here; my vines and my story.
And I have come to hate Rome so. What does he say?
Yes, as usual. But this time he threatens me.
(*He laughs and hands the letter to a* SLAVE)
Well, I suppose I shall have to.

FLAVIA You must obey; to please me, Uncle.

PETRONIUS So it seems. So it seems. Tell me is he still . . . ?
(*He makes a balance of an outspread hand.* FLAVIA *nods*)

14

What a curse we live under.

I would have liked to play with the boy a bit, teach him how to prune vines. He'll inherit them one day.

FLAVIA Perhaps you can come back before the end of the spring?

PETRONIUS So Fabius has gone again? Well now!

What is the name of this barbarian Princess?

FLAVIA Acte.

PETRONIUS Acte! That's right. I *have* heard something.

Well, the Scythians are good for nothing except sex, poetry and intrigue. They are crazy.

I did service there once. I liked them myself.

Fabius will be back in a month dragging her by the hair: you'll see.

FLAVIA How little it seems to matter.

PETRONIUS Come, my dear; we shall dine and I shall prepare for Rome. The country will do you good, Flavia.

(*He puts his arm round her shoulder. Exeunt*)

SCENE TWO

A house in Scythia, with primitive and barbaric hangings.
METELLUS, *the satrap, sits at a table playing a game of dice against* FABIUS, *the Roman General.*

METELLUS Moderation! Whenever did moderation pay – answer
me that?
And with savages like these?
No, Rome is getting feeble and irresolute,
Old in tooth and mind, like our Generals, General!

FABIUS So.

METELLUS I am sorry, Fabius; you asked me to speak my mind. I
am.

FABIUS A seven! You take the point.

METELLUS For twenty years I've been a satrap here,
In one forgotten province after another.
I paid for them, Fabius, with gold – gold, do you hear?
Now this revolt has cost me half a fortune.

FABIUS The revolt is over now.

METELLUS Until next time, soldier, until next time.
I know my Scythians.
I would have burned twenty villages, impaled a thousand
youths,
Doubled the grain tax, burnt the harvest...
That is all they can understand.
And you come bursting in with Roman ideals of
moderation and justice....

FABIUS And countermand your orders, I know.
I know. And I am sorry for it, Metellus.
But the revolt was partly caused by your extortions,
man.

METELLUS They need a good lesson, I tell you.

FABIUS They have had one in the field;
And besides, you have blinded the young Princess, you
tell me.

16

METELLUS My dear boy, if you had delayed another day I would
have put the whole palace clique to death, father and
daughter alike.

I held out in the hope that Amar would fall into my
hands.

But he's as cunning as a boar. He's fled to the hills.

FABIUS Amar? The tribal king?

METELLUS Aye! The tribesman she was supposed to marry! He's
escaped me.

FABIUS Well, he will have to come to Rome to fetch his bride.

METELLUS You are taking her as a hostage, are you?

FABIUS Yes. She is chiefly responsible, after all:
Or so you tell me.

METELLUS And the father?
Why not take him too?

FABIUS He's old and ill; I have seen him and warned him.
But I decided to leave him here under your eye.
You shake your head, satrap?

METELLUS What else can I do?
My hands are tied.

FABIUS You could rule with more moderation, Metellus.
(METELLUS *rises and walks about with suppressed rage*.)

METELLUS I cannot think why they should have sent you.
Everything disqualifies you for such a task.
No, don't smile. I know you spent your youth here and
speak their language better than I.
But you are sentimental about them, Fabius.
This is no place or time for softness and indulgence.
Sentimental, that's what you are!
A sentimental general! Pah!

FABIUS It's your throw.
(METELLUS *resumes the game*)

METELLUS And I shall be left here as usual with only a company of
bowmen.

FABIUS Everything is quiet, Metellus.
Have you counted the dead from the battle?
They won't forget this lesson in a hurry.

METELLUS There, match and game!

(*He bangs down the dice cup and stands up*)
There is nothing more to say.
When do you leave?

FABIUS Tonight. Travelling fast and light.
I will take her with a few personal servants.

METELLUS Well, I shall leave you to your fond imaginings.
I hope you don't run into an ambush.
Amar is somewhere out there.

FABIUS Good-bye.
(*Holds out his hand*)

METELLUS I can hardly bring myself to take your hand.
(FABIUS *bows. Exit* METELLUS. FABIUS *walks up and down. He sighs and pours himself some wine, setting out two glasses. Enter a young staff officer,* TULLUS)

TULLUS I've told them to be ready within the hour.

FABIUS How . . . how did she seem?

TULLUS The Princess? What would you expect?
Sullen, dispirited, but full of fire.
She's not ill, sir.
You wouldn't think so to hear her.

FABIUS But she is blind?

TULLUS Indeed. But she remains a firebrand.
She spat when I said I was a Roman.
(FABIUS *has risen and has given the officer a glass of wine.
They pledge and drink*)

FABIUS Tell me something, Tullus;
Would you say I was a sentimental general?
Honestly now?

TULLUS Who says so?

FABIUS Metellus.

TULLUS Ah, him! What do you expect?

FABIUS Sometimes the wrong people can be right.
The word struck me, that is all.

TULLUS I think you are showing lack of caution, mind you.

FABIUS How?

TULLUS This journey; so far, such a small escort.
I wouldn't.

FABIUS Bah, that is nothing.

I know this country.

TULLUS I know you do.

FABIUS That is perhaps why the word struck me.
It's true I have a sympathy for them.
I spent my youth here, after all, when my Uncle was
satrap.
Golden years for a boy in high Scythia.
The people were content and at peace then.
We were loved.
Then, at least, I was shamelessly sentimental, reading
their love-poetry!
I was fifteen. And madly in love with ... guess.
The younger Princess.

TULLUS Acte!

FABIUS Yes. Our prisoner. How strangely things work out.
(*He laughs*)
I was too timid to go to brothels, I remember.
Her image bound me.
I slept with a sword in my bed, a cold sword,
Always dreaming it was the little Princess beside me.
So the wheel turns.
In the first revolt we killed her sister Metanira;
This time we hold her as a hostage.
Poor Scythia!
Well, enough of this, boy.
Drink and let's be going.
(*They raise their glasses and drink*)

CURTAIN

SCENE THREE

In the prisons of METELLUS. *The Princess* ACTE *is revealed, eyes bandaged, and one arm chained to the wall; two female attendants lurk in the nether shadows while* GALBA, *an elderly and refined-looking councillor, is seated near her on a stool looking pale and dispirited.* ACTE'S *exotic Asian style of beauty is enhanced by great impulsiveness of gesture which suggests a little bit the spoiled child.*

ACTE Go on, make a list of them! Exile, dishonour and
defeat...
The ruin of Scythia and my father's house...
And you sit there and say that fate is merciful,
You sit there like an old maid counting your blessings.

GALBA I only meant that Metellus intended to murder us all.

ACTE Perhaps it had been better for us, who knows?

GALBA I was only talking, my dear.

ACTE You were only talking! That's what diplomats are for.
O when will my father come? Father! Father!
I am so impatient, I could choke with rage.

GALBA They will not let him see you, dear. I told you.
But I have seen him; he implored me to urge on you
Patience and moderation in your Roman dealings.

ACTE Moderation! Since when did moderation pay with
people like them?
No. We must begin all over again, that is all.
We will not desist; we will regain our freedom at
whatever cost.

GALBA O Acte, Acte. You are so headstrong. What has it
brought us?
Three revolts in ten years – all failures.
Famine, punishments and taxes.
And in the last your sister died....

ACTE I know.

GALBA And this time you and your father nearly followed her.

Darling, we are attempting the impossible.
Between heroism and lunacy there is a difference.
Why not think in terms of a treaty with Rome?

ACTE Treaty with our oppressors? You are mad.

GALBA No. I am tired. I see no future for us or Scythia unless we alter our way of thinking.

ACTE Your residence in Rome has corrupted you.

GALBA No.

ACTE Yes, it has. You have begun to think like them.

GALBA The world is a big place, Acte.
Scythia is very small; and you have never been outside it.
There are great forces which direct our lives, not visible from here at all.
Believe me.

ACTE Well, we must bend them to our purposes, that is all.

GALBA I shall say no more.

ACTE Well, that is something gained.
Listen, I am full of resolve despite this mishap with my eyes; nothing is lost.
In Rome we can work, we can spy, until Amar has built up his forces. Then . . .

GALBA Why not let your old father die in peace?
He wishes it.

ACTE He is only tired. In his heart he feels the same Scythian pride.
He would not wish to die a slave, nor will we let him.
Next time we are bound to succeed, I feel it.

GALBA It's always next time.

ACTE Hush! What was that?

GALBA They have come for us.
(*Enter a* JAILOR *who unchains the* PRINCESS)

JAILOR The escort is waiting for you. Follow me.
(*Exeunt*)

SCENE FOUR

*A wood in Scythia. Shadows of trees against a moonlit sky.
The dim shape of tents with lights glimmering in them. A
sentry with a bow crosses and recrosses in silhouette. A log
fire burns in the middle of the stage. Noises off mingle the
stamping of horses with the voices of sentries challenging.
Enter* ACTE *on* GALBA'*s arm.*

GALBA   But it's cold, child.

Put this round your shoulders. So.

ACTE   Listen to the wind in the pines.

I can smell the sea.

GALBA   We are far from the sea as yet.

ACTE   What's this? O, it's a fire.

GALBA   Not too near.

Here, sit on this log. So.

ACTE   Spring in Scythia! Log fires!

I wonder why this man is avoiding the towns?

These paths were never safe for small parties, even in
peacetime.

The woods are full of leopards.

But I suppose he must know. It's odd, though.

GALBA   It's the quickest way.

ACTE   Galba, leave me here awhile to think;

Go and finish the letter to my father and leave me here.

I promise I won't move.

GALBA   If you wish it.

ACTE   Pray do.

(*Noise of sentries*)

Ah! Soldiers! Always soldiers!

(*Exit* GALBA)

(ACTE *sighs and unties the bandage covering her eyes. She
palms them wearily for a long moment, and then holds out
her hand to see whether she can see it. She stands up. The
fire blazes up suddenly and enter* FABIUS)

22

FABIUS Stand back. Stand back.

ACTE What is it?

FABIUS You are too near the fire, Princess. You might set your cloak alight.

Here, give me your hand. Sit here.

ACTE Who are you? Are you Scythian?

FABIUS No. Roman.

ACTE Ah! Then I do know who you are.

FABIUS Fabius, the general; at your service.

ACTE At my service! What a mockery.

FABIUS I meant it politely.

ACTE The Romans are nothing if not polite.

But I admit that you speak our language well.

How is that? Your accent is good.

FABIUS I did so once.

It's rusty from disuse.

ACTE I was about to ask from which province you were.

FABIUS A compliment.

I learnt it in the capital, from the Palace tutors.

ACTE When was this?

FABIUS Long ago.

When I was sixteen and you were ten.

ACTE Did I ever see you?

FABIUS No. But I saw you often riding your white mare,

With a falcon on your wrist;

You wore a gold tunic with bells and a red veil.

ACTE That is right. How strange.

FABIUS Your horse was called 'Firefly';

Your sister rode beside you.

ACTE Metanira. Did you find her beautiful?

FABIUS Yes.

ACTE Yes, she had everything I lacked. So they all say.

Intelligence as well as beauty.

Her eyes were famous. There were many songs about them....

FABIUS I know.

(*A silence*)

I reproach myself for not saving your own, Princess.

23

ACTE Could you have? How?

FABIUS By coming earlier.

I had a sudden wild desire after the battle to ride on the western mountains again, to cross the ranges until ... can you guess?

I reached the great obelisk of Semiramis, your ancestor, That is how I got delayed.

I arrived by moonlight after half a lifetime to read her epitaph by the moon's glow.

ACTE Indeed? She wrote it herself, they say.

(*She recites, half to herself*)

Once I ruled over the Empire of Ninus, from the black Indus river

To the southernmost lands of myrrh and spices.

Before me no Scythian had ever seen a sea.

I have seen four which none approached ...

FABIUS Yes! *And then like music ...*

(*They recite in unison, fired by the poetry*)

ACTE *Rivers I have compelled to run where I wished.*

and *I quickened deserts and made them bear fruit.*

FABIUS *I raised impregnable fortresses upon new roads Where my chariots scattered the wild lions.*

Yet in the midst of all these occupations I found time for pleasure, I found time for love.

(ACTE *turns away to hide her emotion and gives a contemptuous laugh*)

ACTE A Roman soldier who loves Scythia! What next!

FABIUS Yes: and why not?

ACTE Who reads the history of my race by moonlight but does not wish to set us free.

FABIUS 'Freedom is earned, freedom is learned.'

It is a Scythian proverb after all.

ACTE I see why you are slinking out of Scythia by these unfrequented roads.

How Roman!

You feared the people would rise if they saw me!

FABIUS How very Scythian. No, I took the quickest way.

As for freedom!

	You expect dreams to come true as children do,
	Without effort, simply because you wish it so.
	Look at this futile revolt!
ACTE	Futile? No.
FABIUS	It took five years to organize; ....
	Within an hour I had scattered you.
	You cannot face the Roman heavies with such stuff.
	You need pikemen, you need Bactrian horses, longer
	swords, fewer dreamers....
ACTE	Dreamers. Yes, we are dreamers.
	But we will learn. You will see.
FABIUS	Perhaps. We are only soldiers.
ACTE	You are vampires;
	You want the silver mines, the corn, the grain.
FABIUS	And you want the roads that we alone can give you;
	You are too lazy to build them.
ACTE	We are not ants. We are not Romans.
FABIUS	I am sorry, Princess; I have wounded you without
	meaning to.
	It is strange how things turn out, years afterwards, in
	other circumstances, other places.
	When I heard of your betrothal to Amar I could hardly
	believe my ears.
ACTE	It is my business.
FABIUS	Could you, really, marry a hill tribesman,
	So different in race?
ACTE	Amar is a giant of freedom. You will see.
	You have no right to talk to me like this.
	You are taking advantage of me because I am a captive
	and blind.
FABIUS	No. I only asked. Anyway, forgive me.
	You will not have long to put up with my Roman
	manners.
	I am bound for Gaul, and you for Rome.
	But hurry we must.
	We have splendid surgeons in Rome; perhaps we may
	even save your eyes.
ACTE	If you think I am taken in by Roman blandishments

25

However beautifully you speak Scythian,
You are wrong.

FABIUS You misunderstand me deliberately.
I did not...
(*A sudden noise offstage; a snarling and the noise of horses rearing and men's shouts.* FABIUS *springs up. He draws his sword*)
I must see what this is.
You stay here.
(*He places his short dirk in her fingers and exits in the direction of the noise.* ACTE *sits holding the dirk, exploring it, running her fingers along the keen blade. An idea strikes her. She rises and takes a few steps, muttering*)

ACTE Longer swords ... fewer dreamers.
Yes, dreamers! We will see who can dream.
(*She becomes tense with resolution, the dirk held behind her back, her face turned anxiously in the direction of the noises off. Her lips move as if in prayer. Enter* FABIUS *sheathing his sword*

FABIUS It was only a tree-leopard.
It frightened the horses.
(*He pauses and looks at her intently, fully aware of her intention*)
Princess, may I take you to your tent?
It is late.

ACTE You are very kind, sir. Pray come closer.
I have something I wish to ask you.
Are we alone?

FABIUS Yes.

ACTE Good.
(*As he moves towards her she aims a wild blow at him; but he grips her wrist and shakes the dirk out of her grasp, at the same time twisting her down until she is grovelling on the ground in an agony of rage and humiliation. He shouts angrily at her*)

FABIUS Why do they call you 'The Scythian Virgin'?
Is it a mockery that Scythians should seem chaste?
Is it a Roman or a Scythian joke? Which, Princess?

26

Can it be true you never had a lover?
That would be too much to believe.
(*In rage and mortification she beats her fists upon the ground, her head bent. She speaks in a strangled voice full of rage*)

ACTE All that I know of men you have confirmed.

FABIUS What do you know?

ACTE That they are cruel and tied to appetites they cannot master, a venomous tribe.
My sister's husband raped me once.
It was not pretty. I found it easy to renounce such pleasures, if pleasures they were.
I tell you this, Fabius, as a warning.

FABIUS A warning?

ACTE Be warned by me. I am not a woman, not a Princess, not a hostage.
I am Scythia itself which will die rather than yield.
(*She bursts into tears*)

FABIUS Ah, wait, I did not mean . . .
Here, let me help you to your feet.

ACTE Keep away from me those butcher's hands.
Leave me alone. I know my way.
Leave me alone.
(*She rises to her feet and exits.* FABIUS *stands looking after her. Then he picks up the dirk and slowly sheaths it*)

SCENE FIVE

A room in an inn on the Appian Way, somewhere near Rome. ACTE *lies on a bed, propped by pillows. A dim lamp shows her in profile. The* NURSE *is arranging some medicines on a table, front stage.* ACTE *has fever. She is delirious, restless, and mutters confusedly. The* NURSE *crosses to the bedside and feels her forehead, sighing and shaking her head. Exit* NURSE. ACTE *begins to gabble in her sleep.*

ACTE They were standing there, just as I dreamed them.
   The autumn leaves turning and falling round them.
   They said nothing: they simply looked.
   It was like a fresco except that I knew them.
   Afterwards the man in the cloak came.
   I heard his breathing, I smelt his breath.
   Nurse! Nurse! Ah! his iron belt
   Bruising my body. The pain, the pain.
   And how Metanira cried out, such cries!
   'No, No. What do you know of innocence?'
   What could I reply to her? What?
   'You were born a vampire, sister.'
   No. No. Metanira, listen to me!
   (*In her delirium, she raises her arms pleadingly and then sinks back. She gropes for a glass of water, drinks thirstily, and replaces it. She turns this way and that, half asleep. Enter* FABIUS.

FABIUS Ah! You have a fever. Galba told me.

ACTE What is it? What do they want of me now?
   I said I would write no letters tonight.

FABIUS Nor shall you; you must sleep.

ACTE Who says sleep?

FABIUS It is I—Fabius. I have not countermanded the horses.
   You will be in Rome tomorrow. Acte, do you hear?

ACTE Who are you?

FABIUS Fabius. Do you hear me?

28

I have ordered a physician to attend you.

ACTE It was not that she was jealous;
He slew both our spirits with one clumsy thrust,
As a sword could kill twins.
We were so near before, and afterward
I knew we would never meet again.
And now she's dead, and he is dead.
(*She groans*)

FABIUS This is the last stage for Rome.
I came to say good-bye, Acte.
(*She starts up*)

ACTE Who is that? Fabius? Voice with blue eyes.
O my head aches! It is full of falling leaves,
Falling leaves among people in red robes.
I so much wanted to kill you! So much.

FABIUS I came to say good-bye.

ACTE They say I have fever.
Will you feel my head?
Thank you. Your hand is cold.
How beautifully you speak our tongue.

FABIUS You must sleep now.

ACTE Is it really you? Dreams are like waking up,
When you are blind, like waking up!
Galba says you are married to a Roman beauty,
The famous and lovely Flavia–what a perfect name!
It must be so nice for you. . . . Red lips,
And rosy skin and copper hair, so soft,
Like a squirrel's brush–so Galba says.
And Galba never lies. You must be . . .
So happy, Fabius–Roman, General, Conqueror!
You will not come to Rome? You do not love her?

FABIUS I am under orders for Gaul.
I've given Galba my letters to carry to her.

ACTE Were they long or short? Devoted general,
Great dreamer!
Well, cold hearts have the sharpest hungers–
So runs our proverb, Galba says
It was a most desirable match!

Well matched, General. Well acted! Well married!

FABIUS Acte, forgive, excuse, forget my clumsiness.
Rest now and sleep; no more bad dreams.
Sleep, Princess–and so good-bye.
(*He makes some sound suggesting departure, closing the door loudly. She cries out*)

ACTE O Fabius, Fabius, do not leave me so.
I am so lonely.
(*He returns and embraces her*)
Ah! You are here. I thank the Gods.
I am cold, so cold. Rome feels cold,
The whole world is cold, except you.
I hate you, Roman, I hate you, hate you.
(*They embrace*)

CURTAIN, ACT ONE

ACT TWO/SCENE ONE

A room in the palace at Rome belonging to ACTE's *suite.*
GALBA *walks up and down before a table piled with scrolls,*
at which sits EIRON, *a scribe with a stylus, looking up at*
him.

EIRON They are getting angry and impatient.

GALBA Can you blame them? Look how the work is piling up,
And can I get her to issue orders or take an interest?
No. For months now nothing but irresolution, inaction—

EIRON I don't envy you.

GALBA No, I shall have to call her to order, I can see it.
(*Enter* ACTE)
I shall have to risk her displeasure once again.
Ach! Women playing at politics!

ACTE That sounds ominous, Galba! Risk my displeasure,
would you?

GALBA Alas! I shall have to tell you some home truths, my dear.
What am I to do? Work and pleasure do not mix, my
dear.

ACTE What pleasure do I have among these insolent and
haughty Romans? Nothing but snubs and slights.
And I am the Barbarian, if you please!

GALBA We are talking at cross purposes. I spoke of work.

ACTE You spoke of pleasures; the pleasures of captivity!
I forgive you; you are doing duty for my absent father.
(*She seats herself.* GALBA *watches with disapproval. He*
speaks to EIRON)

GALBA Copy out the revisions and attach them.
(GALBA *gestures to him to leave. Exit* EIRON)

ACTE Galba, do you know my sight is slowly coming back?

GALBA Yes, my dear.

ACTE I can see quite a lot now—not letters, of course.
But I haven't told a soul of it—except one person.
Ah! but you know. Now then, what is it?

                I see you shuffling scrolls and looking grim.
GALBA They are pressing us very hard; the new armies are
                ready.
                The young generals are impatient for action.
                Everything turns on the second half of the plan–
                To escape from Rome and join them. They want to know
                when.
ACTE They must wait until I am ready.
GALBA It is easy to say, but suppose the revolt broke loose
                While we are here in Rome? You know the fate of
                hostages?
ACTE Amar would never let it break loose.
                O this revolt! They spoke of years of preparation,
                To make quite sure this time. Now my head is full of
                plans.
GALBA You are having doubts?
ACTE No. I have been studying the politics of Rome a little.
                Looking at Scythia from the outside, so to speak.
                You were right: things look quite different from here.
                I need time to reflect, to think, Galba.
GALBA Is this truthful; or is it that you cannot tear yourself
                Away from Rome and the thought that Fabius might–
ACTE How dare you!
GALBA Here comes the displeasure.
ACTE You are unjust to me; simply because you are in my
                confidence,
                Because I cannot read these letters for myself.
GALBA It is you who are unjust to your servants.
ACTE Am I?
GALBA Very. And now we speak of it, here is another.
                A secret letter under seal from Gaul.
                (ACTE *leaps up*)
ACTE Fabius! Is it Fabius?
GALBA Yes.
ACTE Are we alone? Read it to me, Galba, slowly.
GALBA (*Reading*)
                'Beloved lady, may these words find you well and happy
                Though far from one who loves you.'

ACTE Ah, not with such distaste, Galba.

GALBA I am sorry

ACTE It is not a dispatch, after all.

GALBA He says you met last in the Imperial Garden. Did you?

ACTE Yes.

GALBA That was appallingly rash.

ACTE Yes, love is rash. It was the only place.
I knew every statue there by touch. Read, Galba, read.
(*As* GALBA *reads, a screen opens, showing, against a
transparency, a garden full of statues; the silhouette of*
FABIUS *walks, with arms outstretched, as if blind, among
them, hunting for her. A single note of music sounds*)

GALBA 'So dangerous a meeting place yet the perfect one.
No, I had not intended to see you again; our resolutions
Were unimpeachable. By meeting again we failed
ourselves,
And so discovered one another. How fascinating the
sadness
Of the nightingales, purity of darkness, the fountains
Playing in warm air.'
(ACTE *walks to the corner of the stage and turns to gaze at
the garden*)

ACTE So it was. It was a fatality, like all such meetings. I stood
on an empty pedestal to wait.
(*The foreground's lights fade. The garden lightens*)

GALBA (*Reading*)
'High summer in Rome, scent of the parched earth
Like our bodies; a bed of cool marble, a cloudless sky.'
(*As* GALBA *reads, the silhouette figure of* FABIUS *searches
among the statues; at last one raises its hand. He kisses the
hem of her robe and helps her down. They embrace and move
away back, fading slowly.* ACTE, *watching the shadows
from the front of the stage, puts up her hand as if to stop
them and then advances and enters the gauze and appears
among the garden statues. She holds out her hand, and the
silhouette of* FABIUS *enters to take it. They speak rapidly
in whispers*)

ACTE I have been standing quite still for a whole hour.

33

FABIUS I thought you were a Diana.

ACTE I was. Diana, listening to the night music of Rome.
I did not think you would come.

FABIUS Have you changed? Has anything changed?

ACTE Feel how my heart beats.

FABIUS I did not mean to come myself; and then I decided
To come, to say good-bye. Only for that.

ACTE I have been saying farewell to you in my mind,
Over and over again, for months past.
It has become mixed with my heartbeats now.
And still I am too weak. . . .

FABIUS Why should this happen?

ACTE Do not ask me, tell me why; you should know.
You are the strong one, Fabius. I am the captive, the
hostage.

FABIUS Or else it should have been in other circumstances.

ACTE It could not be otherwise; it was waiting for us.

FABIUS Yes, somewhere else, far away from Rome
With its dangers and intrigues and follies.
We should have gone away together from the very first.

ACTE We could not; we have parts to play in the world.

FABIUS And now I am trapped; we are both trapped.

ACTE Do you regret it?

FABIUS No, but I should;
We may not meet again for years.
Do you hear me, years!

ACTE Years! It will change nothing.

FABIUS O it is unjust, unjust; we were born to be happy together.
Could you break free of me now?

ACTE No. You will always be there now.

FABIUS And yet I am glad that you cannot.
Good-bye, then.

ACTE Good-bye.

(FABIUS *takes her by the arms and draws her away among
the statues. As they fade,* ACTE *reappears on the forestage
in the lights, where* GALBA *is still reading. The garden fades
and dies away*)

GALBA 'So it will go on until perhaps the mind and heart

34

Wear out the problem, gnaw it into pieces;
Or until the words themselves become meaningless,
Like a lost language in a forgotten script.'
That is how it ends.

ACTE Ah, Galba, do not grudge it to me.

GALBA It was not that at all; I did not speak of this.
(ACTE *is suddenly angry*)

ACTE But you hate it, don't you? You simply hate it.
I can tell by your voice; you find it all
Insufferably banal and insipid and disgraceful–

GALBA Please.

ACTE Give me the letter. I know! You are saying to yourself:
'These old maids, when they fall in love,
Behave like double virgins'–the Roman proverb.
I can see it on your face, hear it in your voice.
You are thinking: 'This ill becomes a Princess
With political charges on her to family and country.'

GALBA Yes, you are right. That is it exactly.
You have every right to love, but not to lose your wits
Over an intrigue which can come to nothing.

ACTE I have not lost my wits. I can prove it.
I *have* been planning, along lines far more ambitious
Than you could ever guess, Galba.

GALBA Madam, I am your servant.
I execute such orders as you give me.

ACTE You are just like my father, only worse.
Listen to me now and you will judge
If I have been wasting my time in idle dreams.
In your last dispatch you hinted that Rome
Is on the brink of great changes; you said,
'Great dangers impend.' ... Did you really think so?

GALBA Yes, I did and I do. I know my Rome.

ACTE What do you foresee?

GALBA In fact, in detail, nothing as yet.

ACTE Danger for whom?

GALBA For the gentleman we call X.

ACTE Nero!

GALBA Hush! Yes, suspense is in the very air we breathe.

ACTE His murder or deposition would be a popular move?

GALBA Where does this lead?

ACTE You will see.

GALBA Of course it would! How many senators have been
       murdered,
       Their wives and children spitted like larks?
       Yet they all seem in the grip of a terrible paralysis.

ACTE Very well; here I want to ask you something.
       If *it* happened, suppose someone plucked up courage . . .

GALBA Well?

ACTE Would not Fabius come to power by the very course of
       things?

GALBA Fabius!
       (*He laughs with incredulous astonishment*)

ACTE The Army would bring him in. Who is more popular?

GALBA Nothing could be less certain.
       There are several armies and several generals,
       All more ambitious than he is. No, this is
       Not thinking, it is daydreaming, Scythian thinking!

ACTE Such an act might well help him to power.

GALBA Might is a long word with many echoes.

ACTE Let us suppose–

GALBA Are you thinking of Fabius as Emperor?
       It is beyond his scope; he's a soldier to the core.

ACTE But if there *were* an Emperor who loved and understood
       Scythia and her hopes, it might avert useless bloodshed,
       Another revolt might become unnecessary.

GALBA You take my breath away. Are you perhaps imagining
       A Scythian Empress for the Romans? In raising Fabius,
       You would have to put down Flavia, his wife,
       And dispossess his son–

ACTE Never. By the Gods, never! You misjudge my motive,
       Galba.
       Flavia would reign with him, his son succeed him.

GALBA How feminine! Do you think she will continue to be
       deceived
       Forever about yourself and Fabius? And then,
       What would you do here?

36

ACTE He would send me back to my father. We might make
A treaty which was more than empty promises.

GALBA What do you wish me to say? I shall risk your
Disapprobation once more. Yes, it is all very pretty!
But it has the typical Scythian touch of
Hopeless impracticality. *How* could it be done?
There are a hundred senators who would love to know.
The man is surrounded night and day by guards.
Food tasters hanging at his lips like leeches.
Mr X may be mad, but he is far from foolish.

ACTE He is completely in my power.

GALBA What?

ACTE Yes, I am not joking. You look startled.
(ACTE *laughs*)

GALBA My dear child, I——

ACTE Shall I tell you how? By the strangest chance.

GALBA Not so loud.

ACTE There is no one here. You know the old kitchens
That lie under the royal apartments? Myrko found
them,
And led me there. No one uses them now. They are
Deserted. I sit there in the winter. They are warm.
They smell of apples.

GALBA Well. Well. Yes. Yes.

ACTE The Emperor began to visit me there alone,
Last winter; there is an unguarded staircase to his
rooms.

GALBA Never.

ACTE Yes. He cannot sleep. He has terrible dreams.
He heard me singing once and came to see who it was.
He is like a child, Galba – he enjoys escaping
From the guard. We meet in secret; he is always alone.
Guess what? I make him soup!
(*She laughs*)

GALBA How can I believe such a thing?

ACTE He is good company sometimes, do you know?
He is mad, yes, but not always bad. I have grown
Quite fond of him. In Scythia we should turn him loose

In the village with a tin whistle and a tambourine.
He would be sacred to us, a laughter-bringer.

GALBA But *really* alone?

ACTE Really alone.

GALBA Gods!

ACTE Now do you see which way my thoughts are tending?
And here I need your mature judgment.

GALBA I am out of my depth. My blood runs cold.

ACTE Mine is warm. If such a deed could be of help to us,
If it could bring Fabius to power–

GALBA No. No. It is too much to consider. Acte, you are mad!
This is harebrained; forget it, forget it.
Besides, I am sure you are mistaken; he is watched.
Somebody must know he is there with you.

ACTE No, I am sure.

GALBA How can you be unless you see clearly?

ACTE He tells me so; he revels in the fact.

GALBA It's a trap; be warned, my dear.

ACTE That is why I came to tell you of it; you must come
And see with your own eyes if I am right or not.
There is no haste. We have time to consider everything.

GALBA No good will come of this. Forget the thought.

ACTE Now who is irresolute? No, I insist. It is an order.
It is your duty to verify my statements
And advise me; you have accused me of inaction,
Of lack of thought and irresponsibility toward Scythia.
Here is my answer. You want a plan: I have one.

GALBA I will never let you do it.

ACTE Very well. But first you must come
And see for yourself, Galba. I order you.

GALBA When?

ACTE At the next full moon; I can always be sure of a visitation
then.
In three days' time, Galba.

GALBA But, Princess——

ACTE You will do as you are told. Do you hear?

38

SCENE TWO

The cavernous kitchens in a disused part of the palace;
a fire burns in the hearth. A few sketchy kitchen utensils
stand or hang about. A long table centre has some scrolls on
it. In a corner stand a lyre and a hand loom. An arched
door, back, gives on to a garden. There is the noise of rain
and wind and the flicker of summer lightning. Enter ACTE,
leading GALBA, *who holds candles.*

ACTE Here is the place.

GALBA Brrr . . . it's gloomy; let's have some light.
(*He lights more candles.*)

ACTE They say it looks desolate and decayed. Does it?

GALBA An old barrack of a place. Horrible.

ACTE Anyway, here I sit and weave or think.
It smells like the kitchen at home. Can you see
Somewhere you might hide? There are hangings, aren't
there?

GALBA Wait. Let me have a look around. Yes, here's a hanging.

ACTE I can't promise he will come; but it is about the hour.
From those stairs, up there. They lead directly to his
bedroom.

GALBA I see nothing. They are dark.

ACTE Be patient a moment. You hear his footfall quite
distinctly.

GALBA Shh . . . what was that?

ACTE Only the rain.

GALBA No. I thought I heard . . . Did you not?

ACTE It is full of noises, this place. We will need patience.
Poor Galba. I am always making demands on you.
You will be tired out. But it is worth trying.
I would like you to see how he is when we're alone
together.
Don't be afraid.

GALBA Well, to business: I'll hide behind this.

(GALBA *hides.* ACTE *feels about, to reassure herself about the kitchenware, and lifts a pot on to the fire, smelling it. Then she seats herself at the lyre, playing and reciting as the lights dim away*)

ACTE Galba, do you remember this?

'*Content is careless as a love child is,*
She will or will not as the spirit barbs her
Dive like dove or hover like a hare,
Here, there, gone, nowhere, everywhere.

'*You will never find her,*
Catch her, hold her, bind her long,
Yet she lives a heartbeat in the echo
Of my song.'

It's from your part of the country, Galba.
I expect you've forgotten it. You've lived too long abroad!

GALBA Shh!

ACTE '*Knock on closed hearts, whisper at locked casements,*
Hunt her in dark woods printed by the moon,
In the heart's footfalls or kisses made of air,
Content is here, there, gone, nowhere, everywhere.

'*You will never find her,*
Catch her, hold her, bind her long,
Yet she lives a heartbeat in the echo
Of my song.'

(*A shuffle is now heard off and a voice calls '*Acte*' twice. It has a note of plaintive whining suggesting a sick infant. She takes a candle and crosses to the short staircase, which up to now has been in darkness. Her light dimly illumines a fat and dishevelled figure. It is* NERO)

NERO I heard the music and I could not sleep.

ACTE Can you see to come down?

NERO Acte, I am in pain.

ACTE What have you done to yourself?

NERO My eye is inflamed again. That sty has come back.

ACTE Come down. It is warm by the fire. Come on.

(*A peal of thunder*)

NERO Is it safe? Do you hear the thunder?
I heard all Rome rock in her sleep.

ACTE Do as you are told now! I am not going to stand here
All night long.

NERO Very well.

(NERO *comes almost timidly down the stair to take her hand.
He is anointing his eye with spittle. He wears a mask pushed
on to the back of his head which, when he turns, gives the
illusion of a second face which is exactly like his, only a livid
and phosphorescent caricature. He has a wreath of flowers
round his neck which he picks at from time to time, and he
carries a small pair of sandals in his hand.* ACTE *leads him
across stage to a chair by the fire*)

It was so painful all evening; I could not work
On the poem I'm making for Sporus. Listen:
'*Thread by thread the Hero unravelled her heart,
Step by step he walked into her mind,
Kiss by kiss he spent and killed her.*' There!
But it is no good unless the Minotaur is killed –
A live man, his blood will make her black hair sticky!

ACTE And who will make your music?

NERO I will. The flutes will go . . .

(*He whistles tunelessly*)

Isn't it marvellous? Listen to the rain. The sky is in ruins!
Acte, tonight Sporus mocked me. Poor child. Mocked
his God.
We are all lonely people. The kisses and bridal veils –
They join two emptinesses. Don't they?
Don't they, Acte? Don't they? *Answer me!*

ACTE I suppose.

NERO You suppose! You know! You know quite well.
There should be no marriages, only burials.
We shall abolish everything soon,
All the faces, the sameness, the disgust.
Burn it all down, I say, and in the cleared space
Build something that a God might recognize. . . . Yes!
Vertical, pure, and unequivocally perfect!

See my nice flowers? Smell, take one.

ACTE Jasmine?

NERO Since I wear them my mother has gone;
Simon the Magician was right. She always hated
The smell of flowers, my mother, my *dead* mother.

ACTE Do not speak of her now.

NERO More beautiful than she was in life.
Such blackness and vehemence she has now. Aiee!
When I cry 'Mother' and fall at her feet to kiss them.
They dissolve into a mist. Something is wrong with me,
With my head. I always see a sow eating its litter,
Gobble, gobble, gobble, no wonder I do not sleep!

ACTE Speak of something else, I beg you.

NERO I will. Here are her court shoes.
Look. Such a small foot. In the snow
Her footprints are tiny like mice or birds.
Thank goodness she has gone. What was that?

ACTE I heard nothing.

NERO For a whole week now she has spared me.

ACTE Come, you promised; will you have wine tonight
Or the same Scythian broth my servants make?

NERO Aha. The broth, of course; though I'm a God
I'm a creature of habit too. Yes, O yes. Indeed I am.

ACTE Come to table, then.
(*He seats himself in great good humour, rubbing his hands
and chuckling.* ACTE *lays his place and puts the broth before
him with his spoon and a loaf.* NERO *crows delightedly,
childishly.*)

NERO The wooden spoon! Give! Give! And the loaf,
Good! Good! Now I am back again, *tum tum tum*,
Banging my little spoon. Quick, cut the bread!
When mummy sent me away from her I lived with a
dancing-master,
And his whore and a charioteer and an actor!
Rufus, they called me. I was happy then.
Bang, Bang, Bang, went my little wooden spoon.
'Silence, Rufus, eat your soup.' Aha!
But I was refractory. *Bang, Bang, Bang*.

42

'More soup,' I cried. 'More bread.' There was never enough to eat,
But they taught me to game and whore and master the harp.
Wild days! Now they are gone. There is no more fun,
No more fun in the whole world.
(*He starts to frown and mutter.*)

ACTE What is it?

NERO A bad omen. I had forgotten it. A bad omen.
Someone saw the little son of Fabius with a sword,
Playing in the Imperial garden. Do you know what?
(*He gestures, striking the air.*)
'Now I am general,' he said. 'Now I am Emperor.'
He must have heard his father conspiring.

ACTE Never!

NERO Yes, and other things as well. Letters have been passing
Back and forth to someone in Rome. Secret letters.

ACTE From Fabius?

NERO Yes. I have recalled him.

ACTE Recalled?

NERO I was going to give him a triumph after this victory.
That's what he thinks. But now, we shall see.
If we put the child to the torture we shall find out everything.

ACTE You have forgotten something vital.

NERO What?

ACTE All children imitate the father they adore,
And all their Emperor; you are the father of every child,
Surely you see that?

NERO Do you really think so?

ACTE When you were small with your wooden sword,
Whom did you copy and admire?

NERO Divine Augustus.

ACTE Exactly! Do you see?

NERO There may be something in what you say. I must reflect.
(*He rises and ponders heavily.*)
They say the blind read hearts – can you read mine,
Acte? Look at me.

43

ACTE I see fear.

NERO More, look behind the fear and you will see
The poet I have become, the archpoet of Rome!
When I began to reign, for five whole years
They said Augustus has come down on earth again.
My laws were golden, I dispensed perfect justice,
I spread happiness and security everywhere.
What a pleasure, what an unction I enjoyed,
Watching them fawn and weep and bless me,
Trembling to kiss my sandals and say, 'Thank you,
Thank you.'
(*He gives a sharp, barking laugh*)
Then one day an idea came like an arrow.
It clove my mind, and so I lost my balance
And began falling backward into black space.
It was a whisper which repeated, 'Just suppose
There is no meaning in going on doing good?'
'What!' I cried. 'Is nothing watching, then?'
I felt like a sleepwalker on a high tightrope.
(*He illustrates by a precarious balancing upon the wooden
form of his seat*)
If doing good won't perfect life, make life art,
Then where's the point? What had I done all these
years?
Nothing! No one had changed. Things went on just as
before;
People were just as odious, fawning, stupid.
Man was a slave. Despair struck me, utter despair,
For life must be an art, otherwise it is not life.
Do you see my dilemma? I had exhausted the path of
good.
Boredom, *boredom*, that was all it brought.
Men felt no more, learned no more. Some other way
Must be devised. Therefore, after much passionate
Self-communing, I thought out another way
Of fashioning the truth. It was all that was left me!
It cost me such agony to formulate,
You could never measure such pain in words.

44

Rome pushed me to it. I decided I would build
This other world for Rome or perish in the attempt!
(*There is a sudden crash of thunder and a blinding flash
of lightning. The candles go out.* NERO *leaps up.*)
Acte, where are you? I cannot see you.
I am afraid of the dark. Everything is moving.
Acte, it is my mother. I hear her footsteps.

ACTE Calm yourself. Sit down. Do as you are told!
(NERO *gives a long, sighing moan. Enter the green, phosphorescent ghost of* AGRIPPINA. *It comes down the stairs
and stands staring at* NERO, *pointing at him*)

NERO Mummy, Mummy, don't point at me like that.
I did not do it. I swear, Mummy.
Don't make me do it again.
(*He sinks down on one knee with his arms raised to the ghost
and sobs*)
No. No.
(*The ghost begins to move slowly towards the garden door.*)
She's leaving. Over there.
(*He passes suddenly into rage.*)
By the black God, this time she won't escape me!
I'll finish her off. I'll strangle her! Mummy!
There is an old well full of leaves in the garden.
She would fall softly as in dreams. O Mummy, listen!
But the leaves would smother her voice forever.

ACTE Calm yourself.

NERO Shh! Not a word or she will vanish.
O the long trials of loneliness, the perspectives
Of memory: it rusts slowly, like the sword.
Mummy! It is Rufus, your little son.
Wait for me. You are eating me alive. Wait.
(*The ghost recedes with deliberate slowness, as if to draw
him on;* NERO *follows, pace by pace, shrinking and panting,
as if hypnotized. But he picks up the bread knife as he moves
past* ACTE, *and so slowly exit.* GALBA *emerges from hiding,
shuts the door and bars it. He has an unlit candle in his
hand; it trembles as he tries to light it.* ACTE *clasps her
hands and stands thinking. There is a peal of thunder.*)

ACTE Galba!

GALBA Yes, here!

ACTE You didn't believe me, did you?
(*She laughs softly, speaks almost with elation.*)
You see how easy it would be. You thought I was
romancing.

GALBA I am afraid. You must do nothing, do you hear?

ACTE Of course not; not without consent. I only brought you
To show you that I spoke the truth.

GALBA We must think. We must get away from this place.

ACTE Well, then, unlock the door.

GALBA Why?

ACTE He will come back; he must, this way.
Or he will tap all night, and call for me.

GALBA Come, let us get away from this awful place.

ACTE Let me talk to him some more.

GALBA No.
(GALBA *blows out the candles and unbars the door; summer
lightning still flickers in the garden.*)
Acte, give me your hand. Come. Quickly. Quickly.

46

SCENE THREE

The apartments of ACTE. ACTE *and her* NURSE. *Enter a*
WAITING MAID.

MAID   The lady Flavia is here, madam.

ACTE   Flavia!

MAID   She has something to tell you.

ACTE   Flavia. Why Flavia?

MAID   Shall I tell her you are ill?

ACTE   Why now, at this moment, after so long?
       Has Fabius betrayed himself?
       I cannot see her. Yes, tell her I am ill.

MAID   Very well, my lady.
       (MAID *turns to exit*)

ACTE   Wait, I must. I shall have to see her.
       But first come here and look at me carefully.
       Is my colour high as it should be, my hair tidy?

MAID   My lady is lovely as usual.

ACTE   (*Smacks her face*)
       Very well. So I am looking my best, truthfully? Without
       flattery?

MAID   Yes, my lady.

ACTE   Fetch me my family jewels and the chair of state.
       Quickly.
       (*Exit* MAID)
       She will find me in a style befitting my rank, at least.
       (*Enter* MAID *with jewels and two* SLAVES *with a high-
       backed chair of state, which they place, bowing as they
       withdraw.* ACTE *is adorned with the jewels and bracelets.*)
       Better and better. Now, am I ready?

MAID   Yes, my lady.

ACTE   Admit the lady, and leave us alone together. See to it!
       (*Exit* MAID. *Enter* FLAVIA)

FLAVIA   Princess.

ACTE   You are the lady Flavia?

47

(*There is a long silence*)
Why do you look at me so long? I cannot read your
expression,
Being a little blind. Have you not seen me before?

FLAVIA Yes, but never from so close.

ACTE You have the advantage of me. I will never see you
clearly.

FLAVIA I know that. May I . . . may I sit down?

ACTE It is not customary during an audience.

FLAVIA I did not ask for an audience.
I had a right to come, and well you know it, Princess.

ACTE What have you to tell me?

FLAVIA Much. But there is ground to be cleared.
I hardly know where to begin.

ACTE You may sit. You are a Roman patrician after all.

FLAVIA Can you guess why I am here?

ACTE What has Fabius told you? Is he the reason? Is he in
Rome?

FLAVIA Yes, he is here.
He could tell me nothing I did not know.
Do you think I have been blind to all that has passed?
Do you think his clumsy manœuvres or yours deceived
me?

ACTE Ah, then you know; truly, I am sorry for it, then.
We did not wish to wound you, neither he nor I.

FLAVIA Your solicitude is touching. Let me reassure you.
Neither of you could, were it not for my son.
I have never loved Fabius and now I hate him.

ACTE What brings you to me?

FLAVIA He sent me. In his disgrace, his nerve has failed him.
He came running to me to confess himself,
Unaware that I knew all about you both.
(*She laughs harshly.*)
My laughter seemed to frighten him.

ACTE It frightens me. What sort of woman are you?
Has Fortune despised you, denying you his love?

FLAVIA Long years of servitude and self-disgust–
That is what Fabius means to me. My parents

Sold me to him like a mare. He was paid well to take me.
I have shared his honourable bed for years now.
Ashes, madam, ashes. It is what Rome calls a perfect
match.

ACTE You have come here to humiliate me.

FLAVIA No. To tell you certain truths. You are welcome,
Princess,
To such a man as he is. Welcome.

ACTE Shame, Flavia!

FLAVIA There is no shame in truth. Who are you, anyway, to
judge?

ACTE I have a heart, at least.

FLAVIA Mine has been turned to stone long since. But how
would you,
A wretched foreigner, know anything of Roman values,
Roman styles?
A Scythian *would* admire this type of wooden insect
And mistake it for a man – a Roman trained to duty, bred
to duty.

ACTE Yes! Yes! You cannot take him from me.

FLAVIA The hero of the national response
Sealed up in duty like a falcon's eye,
To be unbandaged only when the Army
Turns duty into murder. Pew!
Could I grudge you such a man?
And now with the first reverse of fortune
There comes the baby in armour, tears, self-reproaches.

ACTE Never Fabius!

FLAVIA He sent me, madam.

ACTE You have never really known him.
Ah – that would give our love a point, a justification!
The man you speak of I have never seen.

FLAVIA We see what the mirror will allow us; even if you
Had your full sight, you would see nothing but
The distorted fictions bred of empty passion.

ACTE How could you bear to come to me, knowing all this?

FLAVIA I tell you he was too cowardly to come himself.
He knew that for the child I would humiliate myself.

49

The child! You have never been a mother, Princess.
It is for him I came, to protect my son, my only son.

ACTE How can I help?

FLAVIA Fabius wants the letters he has written to you.
They alone will satisfy the guardians.
He has already delivered your own to them.

ACTE He gave up my letters?

FLAVIA Of course. To prove his innocence of any conspiracy.
They are harmless vapourings – but what of his own?

ACTE Flavia, they are gone. I have destroyed them.
He asked me to.

FLAVIA O wicked, selfish, empty woman –

ACTE No! It was to protect you that I obeyed him.

FLAVIA Protect me?

ACTE My every thought was for his advancement.
And for yours: you will not believe me.

FLAVIA Advancement! You have nearly destroyed us both.

ACTE Do not be bitter because he never loved you.

FLAVIA Ah, but he does, he did, he always has, Princess.
He found a kind of sensual pleasure in my own disgust.
My frigidity excited him like a whip.

ACTE Please.

FLAVIA You know little of men; there is more than one kind of
love.
I served his lust in silence and indifference when he was
drunk.

ACTE This is what I so hate in Roman women, this cynicism.

FLAVIA It comes of seeing truth clearly, Princess.

ACTE Truth! But he has been true to me, at least, and I
To him – and through him to you, Flavia.
Wait! I was with child by him once.

FLAVIA I know. You put it away.

ACTE *Why* did I? *Why* did I do that?

FLAVIA How should I know? You were too lazy to make a
mother.

ACTE I was protecting your life with Fabius, your son and
heir.

FLAVIA A commendable sophistry for a woman in love!

50

ACTE I never wished to steal him from you, never as a husband.

FLAVIA Self-deceit; you never stopped to think of me.

ACTE You have never lived – how can I speak to you?
We were trapped, Flavia.

FLAVIA I must take lessons in living from you?

ACTE I was never your enemy, but you are mine.

FLAVIA Yes, and Fabius' enemy. If only we had no child.
That is what has killed us.

ACTE I imagined you so differently, spent so much time
Thinking how not to hurt you. Fool!

FLAVIA Yes, you are a fool. If you had really had our lives
At heart, would you, for example, have hatched so mad
a scheme
As to poison the Emperor? That was for us, was it not?

ACTE Galba has been talking to you!

FLAVIA Yes.

ACTE But why should he do that? How unlike him.

FLAVIA I threatened him, madam, with exposure.
He was afraid, afraid of your impulsiveness,
Your lack of sense. He knows my uncle is Petronius
Arbiter,
The only man who still can influence Nero,
The only man who might persuade him not to roam at
night,
Without telling him the reason. Galba knows you all too
well!

ACTE Galba has never trusted me. I promised him not to do
anything.

FLAVIA Evidently he did not trust you. And another thing:
Suppose I had told Fabius your idea . . . do you know
what
He would have done – but instantly? No, you don't!
Your Roman lover would have denounced you to the
guardians.

ACTE Denounced me?

FLAVIA Without a thought. It would be his duty to do so.

ACTE To denounce me?

FLAVIA You do not know your Romans yet, madam.

51

And then – what of me? Suppose your mad scheme
Had succeeded; did you see me on the throne against my
will?
Or did you perhaps imagine *yourself* beside him,
A royal consort from the Scythian marshes?

ACTE Never!

FLAVIA You wanted me crowned the queen of Fabius!
You did not stop to consider the matter at all.

ACTE I would not have changed the sovereignty of Scythia
Against a hundred Romes; can't you see that?

FLAVIA And here we are now, suddenly disgraced by a fiction;
And you have destroyed the proofs of our innocence.
What is to come of it?

ACTE I shall go to the Emperor and sue. He will hear me.

FLAVIA This time you will do nothing, if you care for the head
Of your Roman lover; nothing, do you hear?
You have done enough already. The only hope now lies
In my uncle, Petronius. He may avert the worst.
(FLAVIA *gets up and walks about, thinking*)
The Gods alone know why I should be assailed like this,
And my child's life imperilled by you.
After so many years of patient slavery, too,
By a Scythian vampire! A Scythian harlot!
(*Laying hold of her arm*)

ACTE Enough! do you hear me! By the Gods,
If you address me like that I'll call my slaves
And have you whipped, patrician though you are.

FLAVIA Call them! Call them.
(*Enter soldiers with torches,* GALBA, EIRON, NURSE, MAID)

ACTE Who is it? Galba?

GALBA Yes, Princess.
(GALBA *advances slowly and takes her hands in silence*)

ACTE How often have I said I will not tolerate intrusions
When I am – what is it? Galba! What is it?
Your hands are trembling . . .
(*She peers at him and then begins to suspect the truth*)
It's Scythia, isn't it? Isn't it? Something about——

GALBA Yes, Scythia, Acte. The rumour that we heard is true.

Your father is dead and Scythia has revolted under
Amar.

(*She sits down in her chair of state, crushed by the news*)

ACTE Without a word of warning.

GALBA The messenger was delayed. The usual
mismanagement.
Now it is too late; we are all hostages.
The palace guard is with me here to take us.

(FLAVIA *has been looking on triumphantly. She makes as if
to leave, but* GALBA *stays her with a gesture*)

FLAVIA Well, I must take my leave, Princess.

GALBA Madam, there is also news for you which must be
Faced somehow, calmly faced; the little son of Fabius
Has been taken to be questioned by the watch.

ACTE Ah! Flavia. Flavia.

FLAVIA My son. My son.

(FLAVIA *suddenly gives a cry as she sinks fainting to her
knees*)

SCENE FOUR

A corner of the Imperial Garden with statuary and a full moon. PETRONIUS ARBITER *is seated on a marble chair before a glass of wine and a great bowl of flowers. Noise of laughter from a banquet off.* NERO'S *voice calling.*

NERO Arbiter! Arbiter! Where can he have gone to?
(PETRONIUS ARBITER *growls and, drinking, shakes his head. Enter* NERO *with* SPORUS *grotesquely rouged and clad as a girl. His tunic has bells on it.*)
Ah, there you are! I knew it, my Arbiter.
Always trying to escape and hide yourself.

PETRONIUS Always looking for fresh air. The smoke tires my eyes.

NERO How can you bear to be alone? I cannot.
Didn't you enjoy the music and the doves?
Sporus, come and sit down by us, here.
Poor darling, he's half asleep. Why did you leave?

PETRONIUS I got bored, my duck, I got bored.

NERO You should never say that, Arbiter.
You know it gives me grave displeasure.
You've been consistently rude this evening.
What did you mean by saying that Nero
Was losing his touch, eh? What did you mean?

PETRONIUS I meant that Nero was losing his touch.

NERO It's a rather dangerous way to talk to your Emperor.
I should say it was rather dangerous.

PETRONIUS When I talk to the Emperor, I use the prescribed forms.
When I talk to a fellow artist, my duck,
I speak as artist to artist – d'you take my meaning?

NERO So I am losing my touch?

PETRONIUS You heard me once, you heard me twice.
Sporus, what did I say, eh?
(SPORUS *giggles foolishly*)

SPORUS Eh?

NERO But *how*? You must explain that, at least. How am I?

54

(PETRONIUS *sighs*)

PETRONIUS Well, when I heard you discussing yet another
Circus act with these prisoners, I got bored, *bored*.
Surely you owe us something more original?
But gladiators, lions, wild horses – it's so stale.
Besides, now you have such rich excuses –
A blind Queen who must die as a hostage,
And then your best general convicted of treachery!
Lovely material for an artist to work on. Lovely!
And all you can think of is to have them both
Publicly impaled or chewed by mangy lions. Ach!
With your views on art, it's preposterous, preposterous!

NERO But with Scythia in revolt, what am I to do?
Sit still and punish no one? I have both culprits
In my hands. Fabius clearly did not do the job last time,
And as for Acte – you know the story; you say ach!
And how disgusting all this foolish love nonsense
That Fabius uses as a pretext, as an excuse.
No, no. It is a serious matter calling for reprisals.
What would you have me do? You tell me that!

PETRONIUS Something original; in keeping with your genius, my
duck.

NERO But what?

PETRONIUS It is not for me to say; I am a writer.
We meddle with life from odd angles.
(*He drinks noisily*)

NERO But I count on you, Arbiter, I must know.
As the writer of a story, how would you ... As a writer ...

PETRONIUS If you are going to revise life as you wish,
You must take the artist's way with it.
Why, it's a pure waste of a blind Queen,
It's a waste of a general of genius. A waste!
Besides if they are in love, that is another very
Important factor. Lovers have every right
To meet in a death embrace; to satisfy art, my duck,
Life must be satisfied first. But you know that.
So ... you are losing your touch. Definitely.
Definitely.

55

NERO You really think?

PETRONIUS It's evident.

NERO But that is very serious.

PETRONIUS Indeed it is. Very serious.

NERO But I insist you tell me what you would do.

PETRONIUS I am only a writer; but I know that the artist
Must use life with respect. Life demands that we take people
From their heroic side; what need is there to kill people
Who were born to kill each other? It's waste, waste.

NERO Go on. Go on.

PETRONIUS It would be more subtle to let them both ... well ...
Tempt their own fate, particularly if they are lovers.
Nothing more thorny, nothing more dangerous than love!
It rots the brain and blinds the inner eye.
One takes up heroic positions, strikes attitudes,
Confuses truth and expediency; one suffers,
And in the end one pays for it to the dagger's hilt,
To the cup's dregs; O yes, you can't escape the laws.
A Roman general and a blind Queen –
It could be nothing less than death for them.
As a writer, I know it. But how much better
Death in each other's arms than in the circus!
They would triumph over you and your lions that way!
It's crude, my duck, crude. Downright damned crude.

NERO Really, you begin to annoy me, Arbiter.

PETRONIUS Listen, great artist; such people as your captives
Are so deliciously full of absolutes that it's a crime
To waste them on lions; they are simply aching
To die in the name of love or honour. Push the lever!
Throw them to destiny, but not to the gladiators.
And watch the fun, artist, watch the fun. Watch it!
That would be my way if I were writing them.

NERO Yes, but *practically*, how? If they were characters
In a book, a work of art, not in life? I mean ...

PETRONIUS How elegantly one could assist them to tempt their fate!
I should let Acte escape to Scythia. Oh, yes, I would.

56

	I should send her lover back to conquer it again.
NERO	But he could betray me again.
PETRONIUS	You hold his son, remember; you could name your terms.
	Promise to restore him to favour on the sole condition
	That Acte herself does not survive the campaign.
	Have some wine, my duck, have some wine.
NERO	Do you know, I am beginning to see what you mean....
PETRONIUS	We want reality as she is; we want her in the nude.
	No meddlesome short cuts hastily invented on the spur
	By moribund senators with jaded appetites.
NERO	Yes, the artist's truth in life. I begin to see.
PETRONIUS	Well, here it is, then. We artists should be helping life
	To live out and realize its own pattern. Only if life
	Is served is art served. Do you take me, my duck?
	The order of life is divine, as you are yourself.
NERO	You are a marvel, Arbiter.
PETRONIUS	I write books, that is all; but when they are
	Good books it is because they follow the outlines
	Traced by life itself, of the complex truth of reality.
	Of course, you could kill your characters on the first
	Page and finish with them; but where's the book then?
	Where's your art, my duck? Where's your bloody art?
NERO	But this way anything might happen: anything at all.
PETRONIUS	All the better; people cannot escape the debt
	They owe to life; somehow it will get paid.
	What the artist needs is patience and curiosity.
	You must never be hasty, my duck. One slip of the chisel
	And your statue is spoiled for good.
NERO	You think Fabius would obey me?
PETRONIUS	I think; but we won't know until we write the story.
	It might be more interesting another way. After all,
	There is free will – they might do something different.
NERO	What?
PETRONIUS	Life is various, lovers are unpredictable.
	She might renounce Scythia for him. She could.
	He might renounce his son for her. He could.

57

But either way the artist's purpose is served by life.
This tissue of probabilities we will never decipher
Until the past holds them firmly in its grasp.
The past! Dead certainty, we call it. History!

NERO I believe you are right; we owe it to ourselves
To do something like that with them. Yes!
What my plan lacked was a sort of expiation.

PETRONIUS Implicit in them, though: not only in *you*.

NERO Yes. I wish I could plan like you can, Arbiter!
I'll tell you what. I'll strike a bargain with you.
You put their subsequent history in a story,
So we can compare later between art and history,
What do you say?

PETRONIUS Done. But you will have to give me first
A leave of absence from the court. You know
I never could work in a noisy, dusty Rome.
You'll have to banish me to my Tuscan villa!

NERO You shall go. For as long as you like.
Put them in your book, Arbiter, try and trace their fate;
So we will watch life at work and smile.
Old friend, we will have two forms of art to compare,
Reality and illusion, you in words and I in life.
So we will be the masters of life at last.

PETRONIUS Well said; so I shall begin with her escape to Scythia,
And the sealed orders Fabius must open on the road
south.
Yes, it has its points as a story. Definitely.
Only you could have thought of it.

NERO It's nothing.
I will do my part; it will be exciting to see
What happens on paper and in life. Eh? Life and art, the
twins!
You are a marvel, Arbiter. If they *are* the same,
I shall know that life can be art after all.
What a relief that would be!
(NERO *sighs*)

PETRONIUS Who knows? They may be. I will base my predictions
On human weakness and my Emperor's magnanimity.

58

NERO Oh yes, I am magnanimous.

PETRONIUS Of course you are.

NERO Otherwise there would be no point in being a God.

(NERO *yawns*)

The dawn is breaking. I'm sleepy, Arbiter.

I'll take Sporus in before he takes a chill.

Come, my child, my little partridge, come wife...

Good night, Arbiter.

PETRONIUS Good night, my Emperor.

(*Exit* NERO *and* SPORUS. *After an interval enter* FLAVIA, *cloaked. She sits down in silence at the table*)

FLAVIA Well?

(PETRONIUS *pushes his glass to her. She drinks, shivers, puts it down*)

Did you succeed, Uncle?

PETRONIUS I do not know yet. I have planted the seeds

You gave me. Perhaps they will flower as you wish.

You want them both destroyed, don't you?

(*He sighs*)

FLAVIA Yes.

PETRONIUS This way, they are likely to be; it's a hard thing, Flavia.

Do you hate Fabius so much, after all? Unto death?

FLAVIA Unto death. But I want the child free and the family

Honour unimpaired, preserved for his succession.

PETRONIUS Well. We shall see. Be patient awhile about the child.

I have accused Nero of magnanimity; there is nothing quite

So useful as to accuse people of virtues they have not.

He's granted me a leave of absence.

FLAVIA Before you go away – please! Don't forget me.

PETRONIUS Of course, my dearest niece. I only wanted to warn you

I may not be long for this world myself. But you know that.

FLAVIA Uncle!

PETRONIUS Despina and I resolved – O years ago now – not to outlive each other.

She is ill with the lingering sickness, for how long

Nobody knows; she herself thinks for about a year more

59

FLAVIA But, Uncle, you never meet, never see her.
PETRONIUS There is no need; we write to each other daily.
We are eternally present in each other's minds.
The happiest married couple in all the Empire!
FLAVIA Do not mock yourself so.
PETRONIUS There is only ironic truth, no other variety.
When she dies, it will be as if some old moss-grown aqueduct
Up there in the hills of the mind had snapped,
And all the Roman fountains suddenly ceased playing.
Poor Despina! I shall go back to the villa to write a story
In the time that is left us. Flavia.
I feel you are wrong to hate so much.
Not morally, you understand, but somehow artistically.
There is an obscure connection between the act and wish
Which needs care in handling; one can damage oneself,
One can give a whole world blood poisoning.
FLAVIA I do not understand you, Uncle.
PETRONIUS No. It is badly expressed. Kiss me and go to bed, now.
It is late and I am weary.
(*Exit* FLAVIA. *The dawn breaks as* PETRONIUS *sits motionless*)

ACT THREE/SCENE ONE

A house in Brundisium. ACTE *is walking up and down dictating to* EIRON.

EIRON And so it is agreed.

ACTE Yes. That is all. But add 'In the Queen's name' –
It will give it urgency; and 'on active service', as the
Romans do.

EIRON Do you think you are leaving yourself enough time,
madam?
The full moon is seven days off——

ACTE To reach the Obelisk of Semiramis? Of course, Eiron.

EIRON Amar has sent you the gift of a white mare,
And a costly ring for your marriage to him.
(*He turns over the scrolls*)
Now here is the message about the transport:
They are sending a merchant barque, a big one.
It will lie up off the Cape of Doubt tomorrow night.
We can slip away in darkness and row out...
I must say I am puzzled; everything has been so easy,
It's almost suspicious. Nobody stopping us on the roads.
It's almost uncanny. Here we are in the heart of
A Roman camp... no roads patrolled, no houses
examined.
If the Romans knew we were here.... *Can* they not
know?

ACTE Yes it is uncanny; but destiny must have dreamed it so;
And why not, after all? History is waiting for us, for me.
We are its servants and its motors. It is powerless
without us.
(*A knock without*)
That will be my nurse. See to it, will you?
(*Exit* EIRON. *Enter* GALBA)
Who?

GALBA Galba, my lady, your watchful Galba.

ACTE Did you find your friend at home?

GALBA Yes. The reports are true; there are two legions,
Four others are standing by outside the walls.
In the town, refitting for active service.
They are bound for Scythia. Their general –
Can you guess? – is to be Fabius. He has been here three
days.

ACTE Fabius! How the wheel turns. You prophesied this once

GALBA I suppose he has been sent to redeem his credit
By conquering Scythia. An unlucky choice for us.

ACTE Do you imagine so?

GALBA How should I not?

ACTE He would win no more honours there. No.
Besides, for all we know, he may be bound for Egypt.

GALBA I have seen the sailing orders, madam.

ACTE This time we are a match for him, at any rate.

GALBA This brings me to another thing I wished to tell you.
Beloved Queen, I have come to say good-bye, to take my
leave.

ACTE Galba!

GALBA I ask your permission humbly to retire. I planned it
Long ago, and this would seem the best moment.

ACTE My Galba, what has come over you?

GALBA Yes, my lady. I hope you will not count it a desertion.
My mind was long made up. Many reasons prompted me
And prompt me still; but the chief is that I am old,
Getting old, and tired. I have been preparing a small
Villa and orchard on the coast near Carthage for years
Against retirement. Now I feel the weariness enough
To pluck up courage from it and ask you for your leave.

ACTE Are you so weary, then? Of Scythia, Galba?

GALBA Of everything, if I must tell the truth.
I see so little hope ahead, madam, to be frank again;
I see a black outlook for three things – Scythia,
And Fabius the general, and yourself. There is
No issue to the matter. And I cannot bear to live
In devastated provinces among the dead and dying
again.

62

Then another, smaller reason: a professional one, so to speak.
I betrayed your confidence to the lady Flavia.
Since then I have not been happy in my post.
I believe in your inmost self you are not either,
But your great tact and kindness sealed your lips.
No, I want a few years at peace, to examine my mind
And put my affairs in order. To reflect on death.

ACTE Is it final, then?

GALBA Yes, my dear, it is; tomorrow night at dusk
I'll see you to your ship, kiss hands, and leave you.

ACTE What can I say? How can I thank you for the past?
O Galba, I am truly sorry, I shall miss you.
(GALBA *bows*)
It is my loss, not yours. But so it must be.
(*Enter* EIRON)

EIRON The man in the cloak who was asking for you –
It is the general himself, Fabius, madam.

ACTE How does he know we are here?

EIRON I cannot tell. But he knows. He is below stairs.
Madam, do not receive him; he is armed.
Under his cloak I saw a short sword or a dirk.
Imagine if he should try to kill you here.
Be wise and refuse to receive him, madam.

ACTE I do not think Fabius would do such a thing. He's a
Roman.

GALBA I would be an excellent idea from a soldier's point of
view.

ACTE I do not believe he would. Never.

EIRON Madam, we are at war with Rome – do you forget?

ACTE Not for an instant. No, but if he knows we are here,
It might be better to admit it freely; at least, Eiron,
To find out what he knows and feels. Otherwise who
knows
What might come about? He would have the power to
arrest us;
That would be equally disastrous for Scythia.
But I will see him. Eiron, give me a sword too.

63

We will be matched! The new sword, the long one!

EIRON Do not tempt fate, madam.

ACTE I cannot influence it now – don't you see?

Yes, I shall see Fabius. Tell him to come here.

Thank you. And leave me alone, please, to meet him.

(GALBA *gives her a sword.* EIRON *and* GALBA *exeunt. She holds the sword behind her*)

Strange that I never regret my eyes except when Fabius comes.

(*Enter* FABIUS)

FABIUS Acte.

ACTE Fabius.

FABIUS Beloved, they are sending me to destroy you.

ACTE I know it. This time you will not succeed.

O Fabius, I am afraid for you, my love.

FABIUS I do not want to mock your hopes, but they are ground-less;

You will find nothing you expect in Scythia

But dissension, mutinies, mismanagement, and – failure.

My intelligence is good. Dearest, be warned.

ACTE All the more reason for my presence, then;

I will unite them in a single will.

FABIUS Listen to me; they have given me six legions, six heavies.

Within the month we shall have crossed into Scythia.

Gods, I have not slept for thinking of it.

Turning round and round like a rat in a cage,

Not daring to see you, hoping and fearing.

At last we have had this chance to meet.

ACTE And did you come to kill me – to kill Scythian hopes of me?

(*Throws sword on table*)

FABIUS Yes, even that, in a way; no. Yes, though, yes.

I am going out of my mind. I brought a sword,

I brought a poison ring; in all these odious and tragic

Choices I thought you might die with me.

Acte, before it is too late, abdicate.

I will send you into Egypt. Let us fly together.

Anything! Anything! Anywhere! Somehow!

(*Throws sword on table.* ACTE *laughs*)

ACTE Embrace me instead. Harder. Harder. . . .
Fabius, does my face show how much I am changed?
Surely you feel it in my embrace, a strange emphasis
That is not fear, not despair? Beloved Fabius,
Something has altered in me – can you guess what?
Scythia! I am a Queen now, I crouch no longer
Under the whiplash of events; destiny guides a Queen.
Those mysterious imperatives I inherited
In the hour of my birth – I only understand them now.
An apple tree cannot bear roses. It is not in nature.
It is so wonderful to comprehend at last, such a relief.
Of course, the old heartbreak will be always there –
My love for you – and nothing changes that. Yet, yet,
I am stronger than myself, as strong as Scythia now.
Memories of my father, of Metanira my sister hover
over me,
The old hurts, the old remembered caresses like
wounds!
I must be true to them now; even though I shall never be
As great as my sister – my father was right to prefer her,
Even though it made me suffer; I knew he was right.
I was nothing to her; her eyes were so dazzling
That I was glad to lose my own and with them all
comparisons.
But now I am in her place I must not falter.
Do you see?
FABIUS Ah, no. No. There must be something to be done,
Something to change the pattern of this grotesque
misfortune.
ACTE Is duty no more use to you as a shield against life?
It is my only refuge now, and Scythia's.
FABIUS Duty!
(*He laughs*)
ACTE It would have been so once.
FABIUS Self-indulgence! You talk like an actress.
What of a soldier crushed by the excesses
Of lies, of a tissue of foolish lies? Lies!
Duty! Honour! Emperor!

65

(*He spits*)
That for your duty. It is my child that rules me.
That is what hurts me here in all of this.
I want him safe.
And you, Acte, you.

ACTE Simon the Magician called us star-crossed once,
But I wonder if he saw this chapter?
You will have the child back safe and sound, Fabius;
You will get him back somehow. I know it.

FABIUS I thought at first to make a pact with you,
To poison a wine cup so at least we might die
Tranquilly in each other's arms; or, if not,
To run you through the body and then myself. . . .
Gods, Gods. A Roman solution, at least.

ACTE What would that solve? It would belittle fate.
Besides, our common guilt would be assumed.
No, at the first full moon my generals will meet me
At the Obelisk of Semiramis; they will drink the Queen's
blood
From the gold crater, they will swear and kneel.
Scythia, Fabius, Scythia – that is all I have left.
Already the sixth legion is reeling under their blows;
Already you, my only and enduring love, seem faded;
Are to become part of this terrible pageant.
(FABIUS *pours wine with shaking hands. Drinks and laughs
harshly*)

FABIUS How differently things turn out; I had thought
You would have greeted our death with rapture –
That, dying, I would recite the epitaph of Semiramis
Until we fell asleep. *Gelden buk var; gelden vien dirralim.*

ACTE No. Don't. Don't!

FABIUS You cannot have forgotten it?*Vien dirralim akbar.*

ACTE You must not speak Scythian. No. I will not have it.
It will destroy everything, everything, Fabius!

FABIUS *Akbar el kasim casimir.*

ACTE No! No!

FABIUS What does it matter now? Who will endure
To be worthy of her? We are the trash of history

66

In a rotten Empire staggering to its doom.
Ah, but with a knifestroke I could cut the girths
And set the wild horse free.
Acte! is this all you have to say?

ACTE Give me to drink. My ears are buzzing. My throat
Is parched. Fabius . . . I know why you hesitate,
I know the thoughts which cross your mind.
But you will not do it; I know that too. Poison
Would solve nothing. Let me drink.
Look, I pledge you in the old fashion.
'In wine marches courage,' says the Scythian poet,
'In wine walks love.' Come pledge me also, Fabius,
For who can tell when next we'll meet, if ever,
How nobly history plans, but how sadly;
A great mansion with many, many doors,
And we small people, the heroes of the action,
Like the inhabitants of a doll's house. Who invented us?
Why are we here? Whither shall we vanish?
(FABIUS *sits at table*)
Yes, we can oppose history, bend history,
But only human duty dare stare history in the face!
Love by it we must, live by it we must;
There are no options taken out with fate.
'Smoothly run the course of the sword' – I am quoting
again –
'Easily breaks the heart.' How sweet to hear the
Scythian tongue
Upon your lips again. I could not bear it.
Fabius, you must leave me now, my dear.
(*She touches his shoulders*)
Embrace me as a keepsake. Never forget.
(*Exit* FABIUS. *She stands. Enter the* NURSE)

NURSE He has left, madam. They have bolted the gate now.
We will be safe from intrusion.
The ambassadors from Amar have arrived
With the marriage gifts.

ACTE Admit them. I am ready for them.
(*She stands with hanging head*)

67

SCENE TWO

A room in a country villa far from Rome. PETRONIUS *is
seated at a marble-topped table with his arms bare and
spread before him. A* BARBER *with a case of razors stands
over him, taking a keen professional interest in the incisions
he has made in the wrists. The scene is played in a completely
matter-of-fact tone of voice. The two men might be playing
chess.* PETRONIUS *reaches for a goblet of wine which stands
beside a bottle on the marble table. The* BARBER *catches his
hand.*

BARBER Ah, no! Try and keep them as still as possible. Let me!
You'll spoil my handiwork. There!   . .
(*He gives* PETRONIUS *a drink, holding the goblet to his lips.
The patient drinks, and sighs with pleasure.*)

PETRONIUS What is better than the good red wine of one's own vineyard?
Have some yourself, surgeon. Blood of Tuscany, they
call it!

BARBER No, thank you, not yet.

PETRONIUS Come, man. Help me to celebrate the new vintage.
This year the harvest was exceptional, magnificent.
We must drink the old wine to honour the new,
You take your job too seriously, much too seriously.
(*He gestures*)

BARBER It is no good unless you stay relatively still, sir.
See, the lateral incisions are very fine.
The blood comes slowly, but nevertheless, if you
move...

PETRONIUS What – if I move. What can happen?

BARBER You will quicken the flow unduly. Be patient, sir.
You do not want to die untowardly, suddenly, all at
once,
Like a sacrificial ox with its windpipe slit?

PETRONIUS What! And ruin by one vulgar slip of the knife

68

	A lifetime's reputation for measure and elegance?
	Of course I don't. I should have you whipped!
BARBER	Quite. Then be ruled by me. Have confidence, sir.
	In this way you will last till midnight, as you wish.
PETRONIUS	The moon is full tonight – a harvest moon.
	The first warm chill of autumn will have touched the air.
	This is the season I love the most of all.
BARBER	Yes.
PETRONIUS	I feel the dead weight of mortality
	Lift from my heart, the full wine cup
	Of human experience running over. Tester there!
	(*Enter* SLAVE)
	How goes that banquet, will you tell me?
TESTER	The wine is circulating, master, the second jar.
PETRONIUS	Already? That is good work.
TESTER	Your guests are happy. All will be well.
	Soon the music will start.
PETRONIUS	Open the outer doors, will you? I want to hear
	The laughter as the wine rises in their voices
	To bloom in conversation, the play of anecdote and wit!
	Let me hear them laugh!
TESTER	Yes, master
	(*Exit* SLAVE)
PETRONIUS	When does the bath come, surgeon? I am anxious
	For the luxury of lying down. My bones are old, you know.
BARBER	A little later. All in good time, sir, all in good style!
	The water is heating now. Let me massage the arms a little,
	So you do not feel a cramp. So.
PETRONIUS	That's better. Another drink, my friend. I want to toast.
	Some old memories.
BARBER	Very well. Stay still, sir.
	(*The* BARBER *gives* PETRONIUS *another drink*)
PETRONIUS	The Blood of Tuscany! Drops sacred to Adonis.
	Have some blood, surgeon – some *real* blood. Aha!

BARBER   Later, when I have settled you down in the bath, sir.

PETRONIUS   You are too serious, man. You will get on in your
            profession, I fear.

BARBER   It is a somewhat delicate business, sir.
            To arrange for the perfect death. In fact, if I
            May say so, it partakes of art. Don't think me
            Presumptuous, but I have never disappointed a
            gentleman yet.
            I have always given satisfaction.
            (*A burst of laughter from the banquet without*)

PETRONIUS   Aha! Good! Good!
            (*More laughter*)
            They are gathering speed; the sails are filling.
            A harvest banquet is always the best of the year.
            Well, my affairs are all in order, like the vineyards!
            Ah ... that hurt me a little; for the first time.

BARBER   I cut a little more deeply, to open the way.
            Your age makes the blood slower, sir.

PETRONIUS   Well, I am in your hands, great artist!

BARBER   Shall I call for some poetry to be spoken?
            Or for a philosopher to amuse your mind
            With some conundrums of geometry or science?

PETRONIUS   No.

BARBER   That is how many gentlemen prefer it.

PETRONIUS   I always had simple tastes.

BARBER   So long as you do not become despondent, sir.
            Some gentlemen have regrets, leaving their friends
            behind.

PETRONIUS   I have everything to gain and nothing to mourn;
            I shall leave nobody behind to really care,
            And I shall find somebody who does in that quiet valley,
            With its wintry vineyards and ghostly olive trees.
            I only regret that I am so impatient.
            You must excuse me. . . .

BARBER   You will get into the rhythm in a while.
            But it must go slowly with the maximum of style.

PETRONIUS   You are right! Style is the word. That is what the world
            lacks!

(*Enter* SLAVE)

What is it, Tester? We are busy.

TESTER Your niece has arrived, sir.

PETRONIUS My niece! Damnation! Flavia!

Why on earth should she come after so long?
At such a time? She must not see me like this.

BARBER Do not fear. I'll bind you, sir.

PETRONIUS No. I won't see her. Why should I see her?

BARBER But this is a family tie, sir. You know you must.
As a gentleman, you must follow form.
(PETRONIUS *groans*)
Leave it to me. I can slow it down.

PETRONIUS Yes, you are right. I must. Give me a drink, then.

BARBER Give us a few moments before admitting her.
(*Exit* SLAVE. *The* BARBER *binds up the wrists of*
PETRONIUS *and wipes down the table with a sponge*)
There, you see? It was quite easy. Everything is proper.
There is no cause for alarm.
(*Laughter from the banquet. Enter* FLAVIA)

PETRONIUS Welcome, dear niece.

FLAVIA Uncle.

PETRONIUS We did not expect you.

FLAVIA I heard that Despina was dead. I hurried from Rome.
O my uncle, must you really make this choice?

PETRONIUS Need I answer you? You look upon a happy man,
Flavia!
Let us have no long faces, my dear. You did not come
To spoil everything and throw death into disarray?
(*A burst of laughter*. FLAVIA *winces*)

FLAVIA What is that?

PETRONIUS A harvest banquet in honour of the new wine.
Thirty of the biggest drunkards in all Tuscany
Have come to feast my leave of absence in the old style.

FLAVIA Is there nothing I can do for you?

PETRONIUS For me, nothing; for yourself, a great deal.
You have your life to live as yet, my dear.

FLAVIA What life? What life?

PETRONIUS How do you mean – 'what life'? Wretched creature!

71

FLAVIA Do you know nothing, then? Is it possible?
All the months you have been here without news?
PETRONIUS You know what country life is. Besides, I hate news.
FLAVIA Acte? Fabius?
PETRONIUS Has something happened to them all?
FLAVIA It is incredible that you should not know.
PETRONIUS Darling, wait! I have been dealing with them on paper.
Art is not life, and life was not my concern.
I have finished their story in my book; that is enough.
There, I know what happened; it did not fall out as I
first planned.
I became indulgent to them. She abdicated and fled
with him.
They lived in exile and disgrace in Egypt, banished
both.
A new dimension opened in their love. They were
penniless,
But together. They forged a new life of hardships. Yes.
So a child was born, and Acte–
Somehow the solution is not the one I sought.
(*A burst of laughter*)
FLAVIA Ah, you are mocking me!
PETRONIUS No. I swear it! I am recounting my book to you!
FLAVIA You could not do it if you knew the truth.
PETRONIUS Tell me the truth, then. It must have fallen out
As you planned it. Did the trap not work? Both dead?
FLAVIA Bid the surgeon go.
PETRONIUS Will the bandages hold?
BARBER Yes, sir. For a while. But not too long.
PETRONIUS Leave us a while together.
BARBER Very well, sir.
(*Exit* BARBER)
PETRONIUS What is the truth, Flavia?
(*A burst of laughter.* FLAVIA *covers her ears. Then she gets
up and walks about.*)
What of Acte?
FLAVIA She is dead.
PETRONIUS Of course; one could see she would lose her life.

72

Scythia gaped before her like an open furnace.
So the plan worked after all! You should be happy at
least.

FLAVIA   She thought the Romans could be beaten by a handful
Of dreamy peasants from a bog, spouting poetry.
You were right – people will tempt their fate.

PETRONIUS   Of course; one could see she would lose her life
In some thoughtless and tragic pageant. She belonged to
art!
But that is how it should be; what have you to regret?
You wanted it so. I could see it written on your face.

FLAVIA   Yes. I did want it so.

PETRONIUS   And what of Fabius?

FLAVIA   He defeated them quite easily, as you guessed he
would.
They would not submit, the young generals and the
Queen.
They retreated for the final battle to the great
Obelisk of Semiramis. They all died.
And Fabius accomplished his imperial task.
In a way, it was like the final humiliation.
Indeed, almost more like one of your stories than
reality;
He cut her head off and carried it back to Rome.

PETRONIUS   So *he* did not die? The plan went wrong!

FLAVIA   Wait. His campaign has made him rich and famous,
Cherished and beloved. All our properties have been
Restored again, and the family credit. Everything!

PETRONIUS   Bravo! That is something.

FLAVIA   Yes, but it crushed him. It crushed Fabius, Uncle.
The fame he bought at such a price. He has become
now
A hopeless drunkard; he will never hold a command
again.
Probably he will die. He has destroyed himself.

PETRONIUS   Hum! That is a twist I would not have foreseen; how
cunning
Life is. Art limps behind it, trying to catch up.

73

No, I would have put it to you another way.
Altogether closer to life as well as to art.
I should say that when she got back she found
Her deception complete, the Scythian forces in complete
Disarray, mutinous and dispersed; disorganized.
All the money had been wasted on useless arms
Or embezzled by the tribal chiefs. Despair
Entered her heart. Yet she could not look back.
Do you see what I mean? She married Amar and tried
To cement the tribes together for the revolt.
Then she discovered to her horror that her father
Had been poisoned by him. Wait. Let me go on.
He had been old and irresolute; the tribal kings
Pressed Amar for action, drove him to declare the revolt.
He had to act; he was between two forces.
The whole business went off awry....
Give me a drink, Flavia.
(*He drinks deeply, sighs*)
And then, as the final touch, you could have
Amar betray her; he cut off her head to save his own....
You look impatient. I am only writing in my head.

FLAVIA We do not know for certain.

PETRONIUS We will never know for certain. Yet I am sure
That is how it was, in art if not in life.
But at least the child was restored to you
As I said it would be? That at least came right?

FLAVIA Yes.

PETRONIUS Well?

FLAVIA The child is mad, Uncle, after what he endured.
He is just as beautiful, only now he is mad.

PETRONIUS Mad! But this is sheer genius!

FLAVIA He can only repeat, over and over again, a single phrase:
'Heroism is divine. My father is a God.' Over and over again.

74

PETRONIUS   My father is a God! How limited the human imagination
is!

The catalogue of human pain is fathomless. We try to
Circumscribe it with our poems and stories. Mad!
Flavia, embrace me! How terrible beauty is!
(FLAVIA *flies into his arms and sinks slowly to the ground
until she is kneeling*)
And so at last we see her naked. Life!
Stripped to the quick of truth.
So things close in on us at last, the great
Houses fall into disrepair and ruin, guilts
Rust the blood, invade the guiltless nerves.
Slowly the fountains pause, the nightingales cease
Murmuring; the chapter ending will begin another. . . .
And you, Flavia? You have lived so much, yes,
But you have never *worked* at life, never once.
Said 'Yes' to life, 'Yes' and again 'Yes'.
Like all of us, you have connived with time.
One day you will see that death is not merely
To be 'died' but to be *achieved*. Despina
Taught me that; I simply pass the message on.
Yes it *is* possible to become an adept of reality.
(*A burst of laughter from the banquet. Enter the* BARBER)

BARBER   It is time, sir.

PETRONIUS   I know. The bandages are slipping.

BARBER   The bath is ready.
(PETRONIUS *motions to the* BARBER *to be silent. He strokes
the head of* FLAVIA)

PETRONIUS   You remember the stories I used to tell you as a child?
The fables of heroes and giants and lovers? Well!
I will tell you one now if you will help me.
Come and sit beside me, Flavia, will you?
There is one story I have never told a living soul:
I have been saving it for you for a long time. Come with
me!
(*The* BARBER *undoes the bandages; a burst of laughter*)
Life is so good when it is leading somewhere.
Come, dry your tears, child, and hear my story.

75

(*They help him to his feet and lead him slowly off.*)
And bring the wine!
(FLAVIA *picks up the wineglass and rejoins him. Slowly the candle fades into darkness. Music.*)

CURTAIN

Max Eckhard as Fabius, Joana Maria Gorvin as Acte

Act One, Scene 5

Eduard Marks as Galba, Joana Maria Gorvin as Acte, Max Eckhard as

Act Two, Scene 1

Joana Maria Gorvin as Acte, Werner Hinz as Nero

Act Two, Scene 2

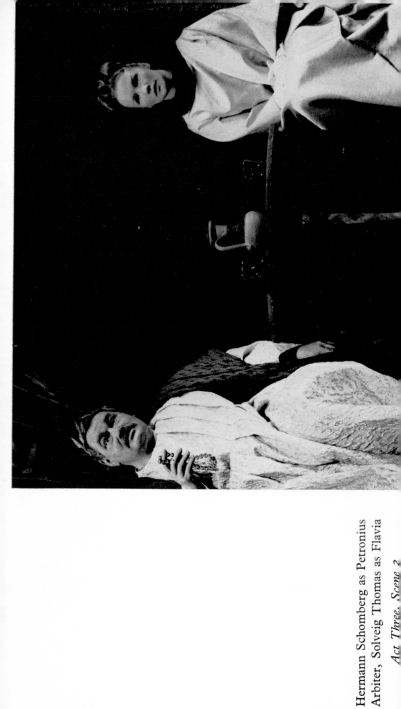

Hermann Schomberg as Petronius
Arbiter, Solveig Thomas as Flavia

Act Three, Scene 2